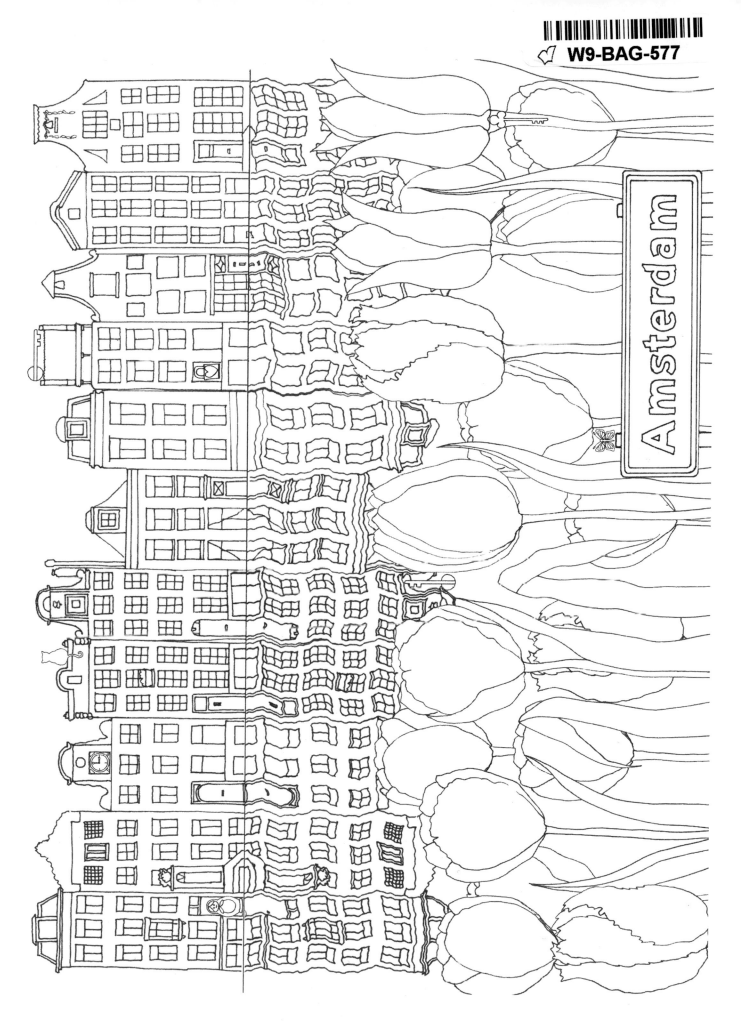

Amsterdam

1

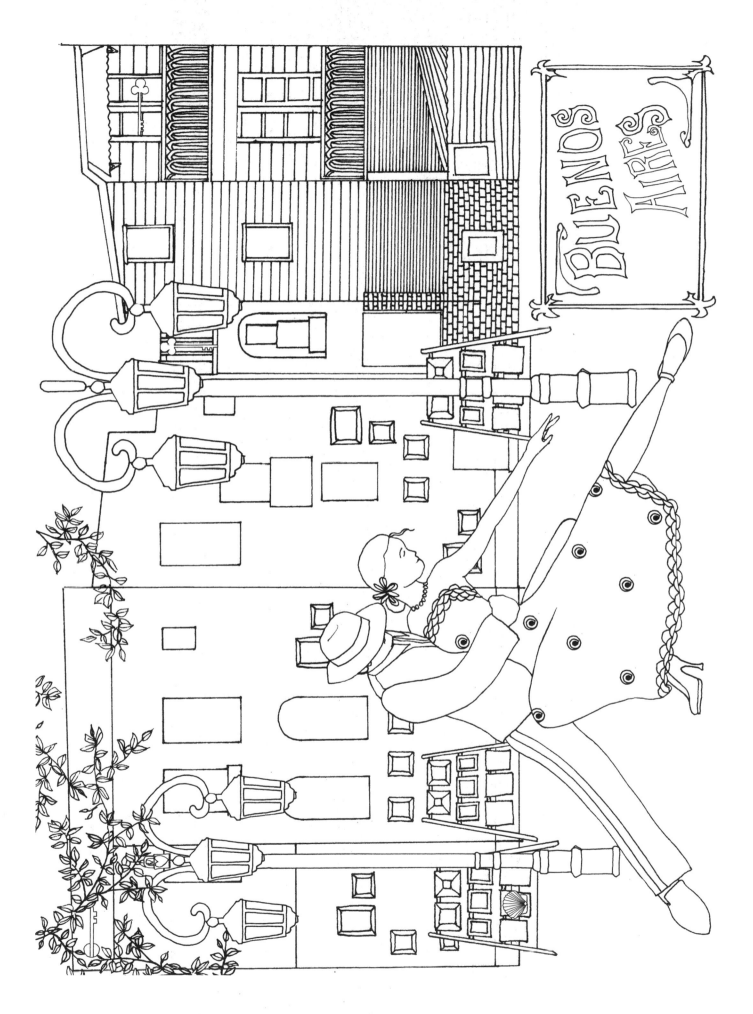

4

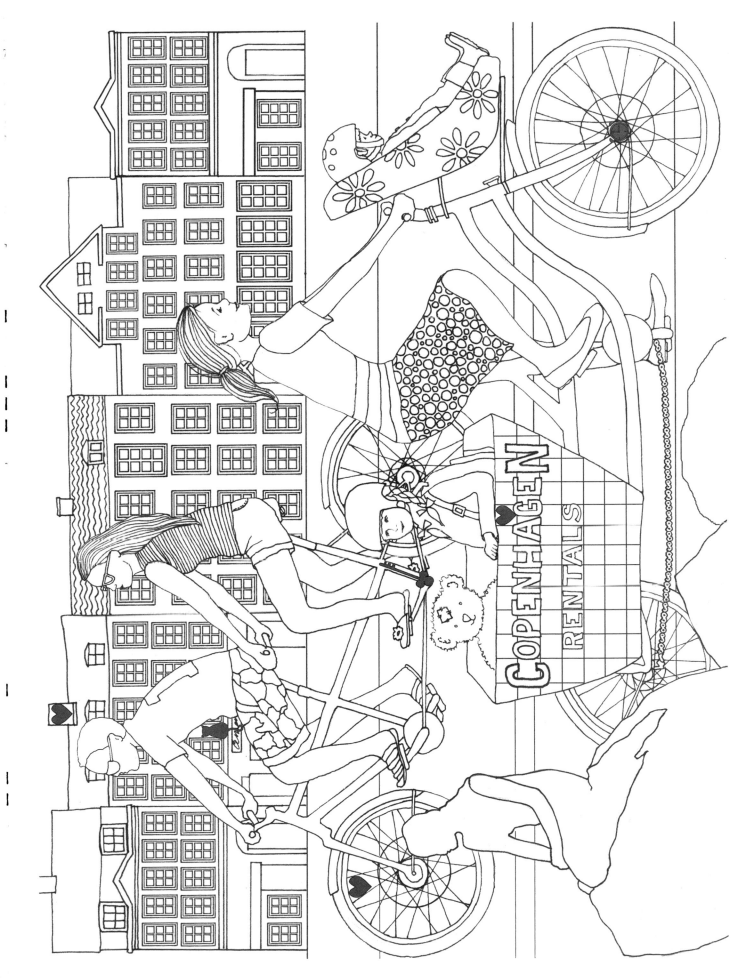

The Red Fort Delhi

THE ROYAL MILE

THE ROYAL MILE

EDINBURGH

9

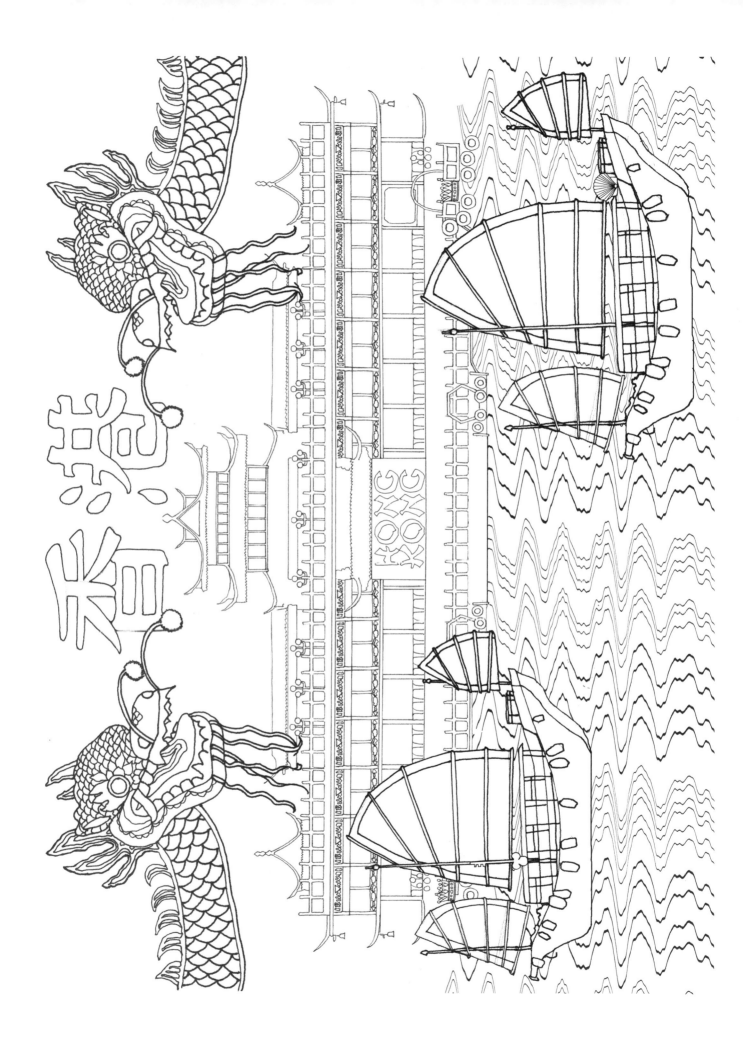

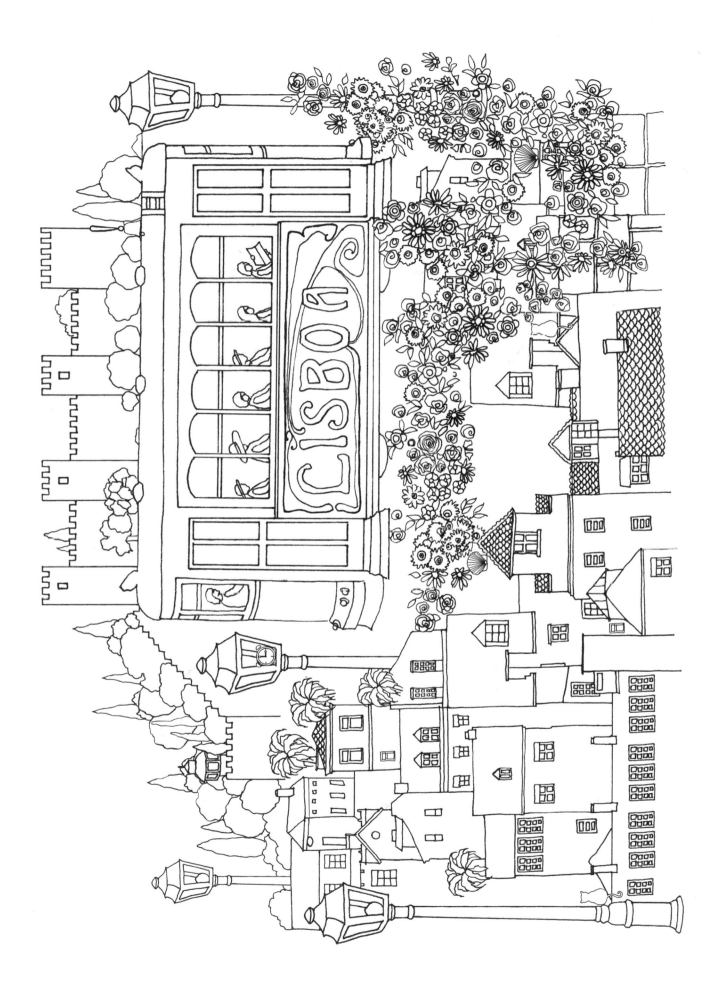

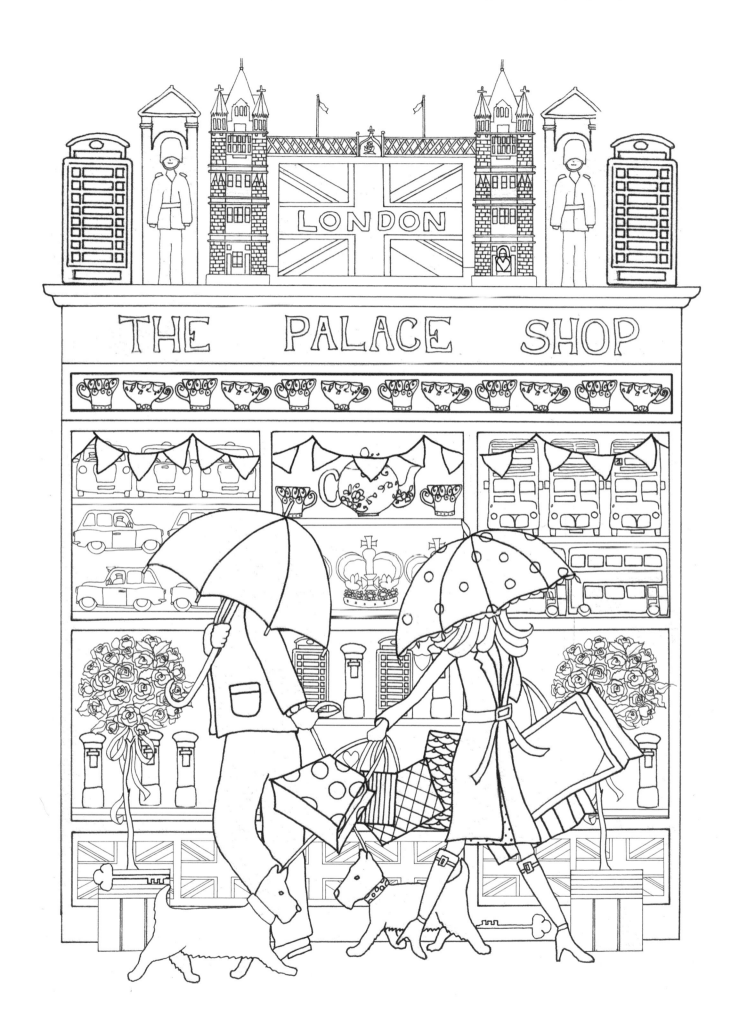

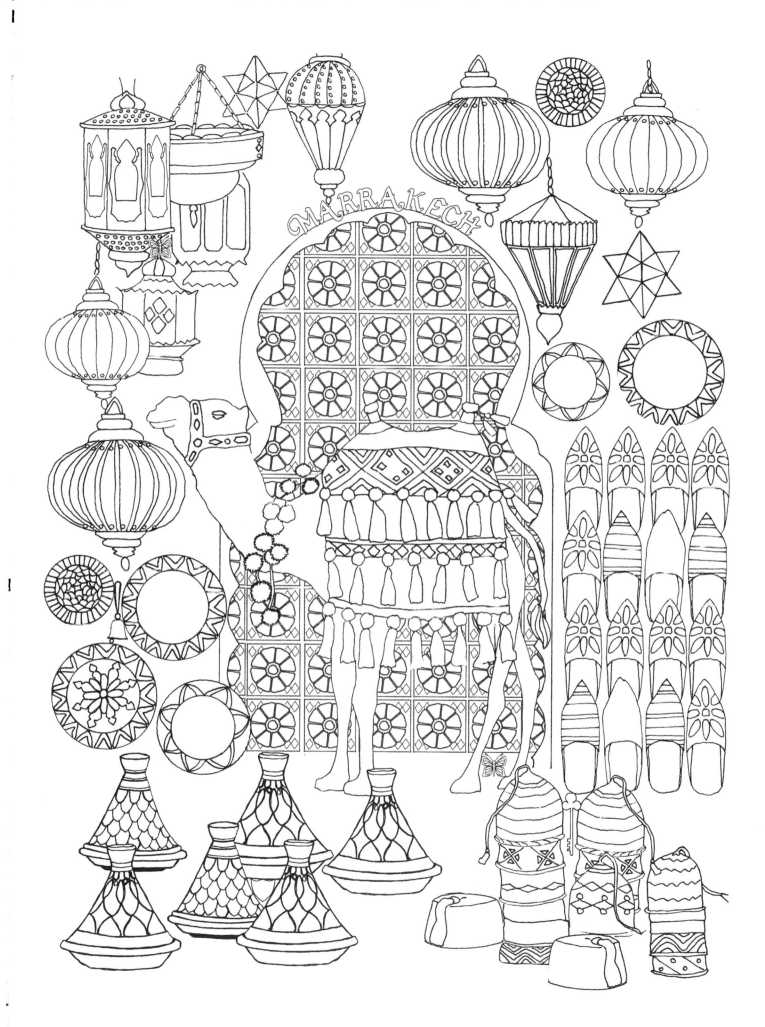

MARRAKECH

19

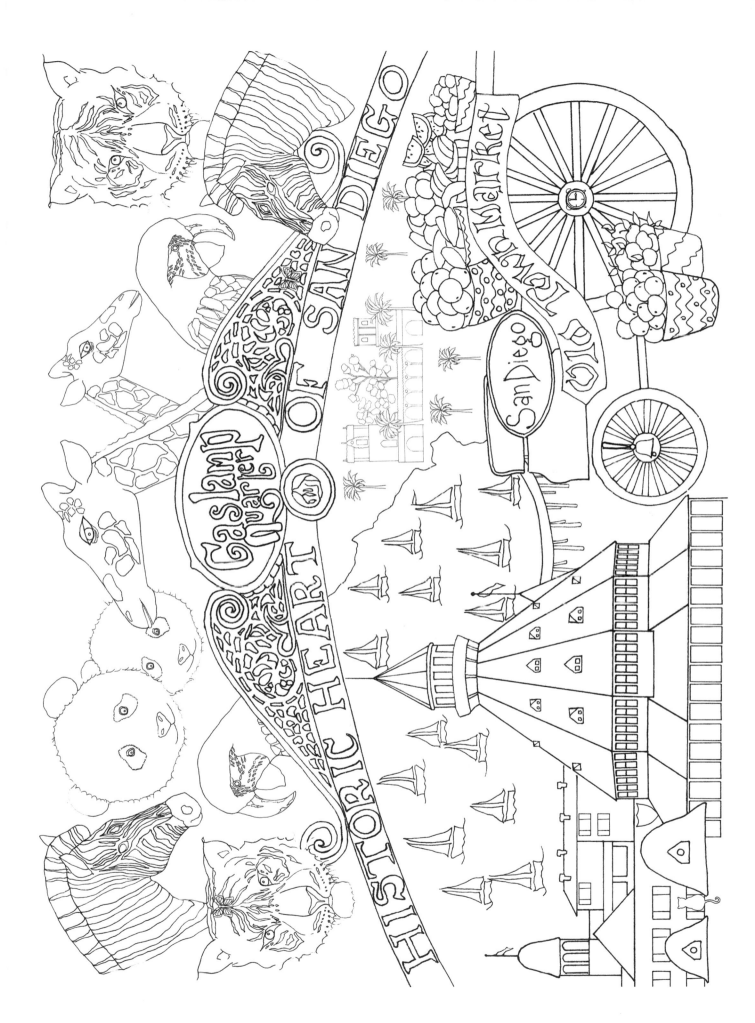

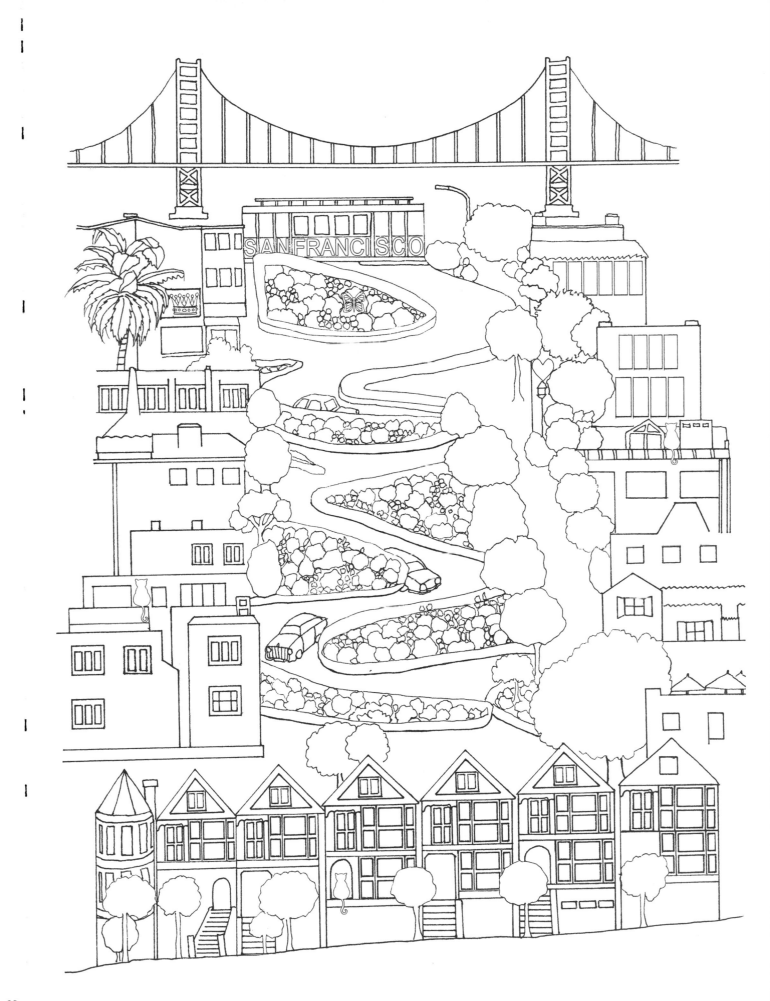

24

ST. PETERSBURG

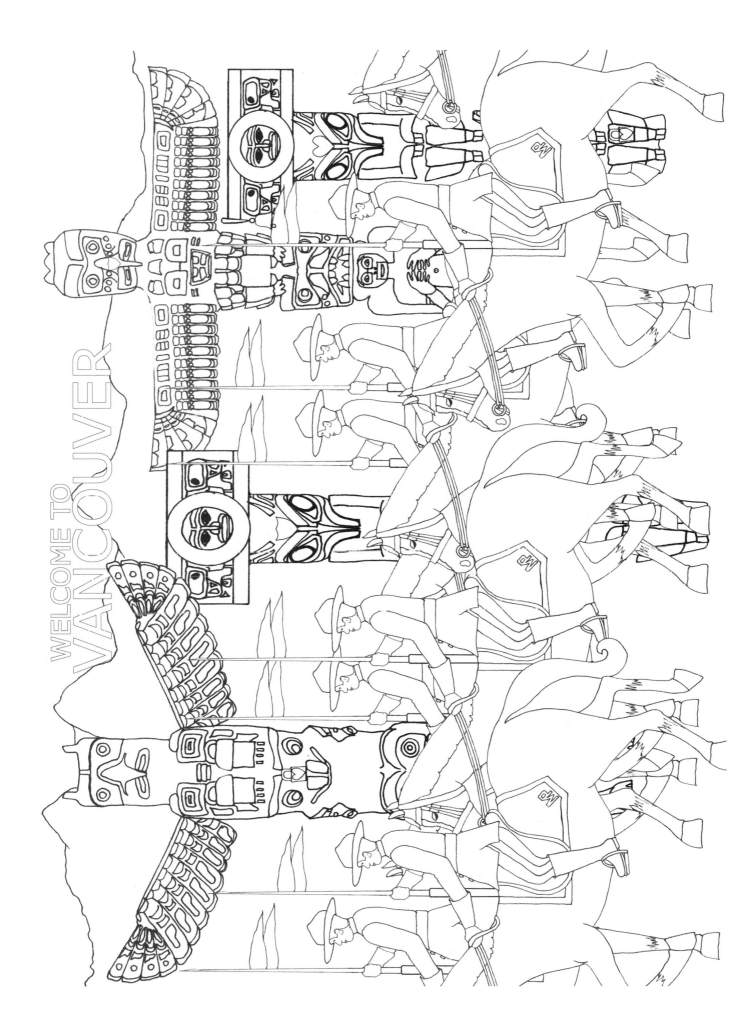

28

SOLUTIONS FOR CityScapes

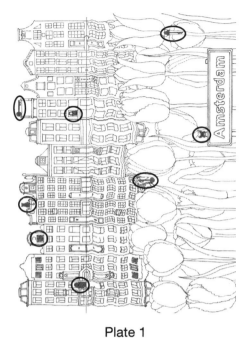

Plate 1
Butterfly, Cat, Clock, Decorative Key, Padlock, Round Key (2), Russian Doll

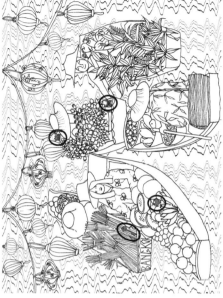

Plate 2
Butterfly, Crown, Heart, Round Key

Plate 3
Cat, Clock, Crown (2), Shield (3), Round Key

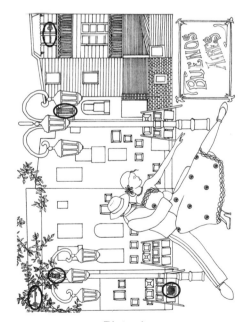

Plate 4
Decorative Key (2), Padlock, Round Key, Shell

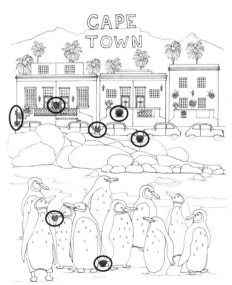

Plate 5
Clock, Heart (2), Round Key, Shell (3)

Plate 6
Butterfly (2), Clock, Padlock (2), Round Key (2), Russian Doll, Shield

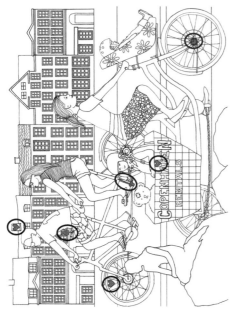

Plate 7
Cat, Clock, Decorative Key,
Heart (3)

Plate 8
Butterfly, Crown, Decorative Key (2),
Heart, Russian Doll

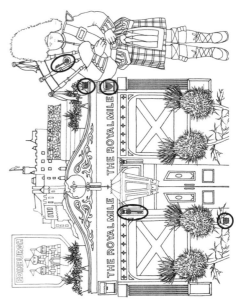

Plate 9
Clock, Crown,
Round Key (2), Shield

Plate 10
Bell, Crown, Cat (2), Clock,
Padlock, Russian Doll

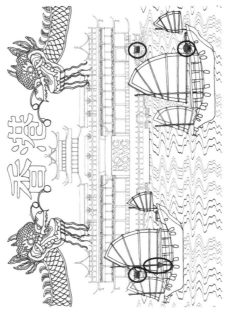

Plate 11
Decorative Key, Crown (2), Shell

Plate 12
Heart (3), Shell, Shield,
Round Key, Russian Doll

CITYSCAPES

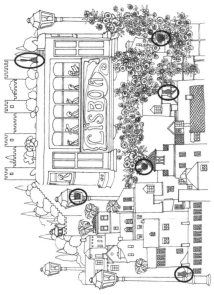

Plate 13
Bell, Cat (2), Clock, Shell (2)

Plate 14
Decorative Key (2), Heart,
Padlock, Shield

Plate 15
Butterfly (2), Clock, Crown, Heart

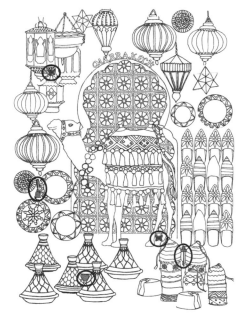

Plate 16
Bell, Butterfly (2),
Decorative Key, Sheild

Plate 17
Crown, Decorative Key (2),
Padlock (2), Shell (3)

Plate 18
Clock, Decorative Key,
Heart (2), Padlock

CITYSCAPES

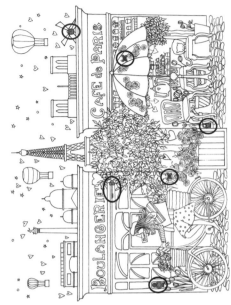

Plate 19
Butterfly (2), Clock, Decorative Key,
Padlock, Russian Doll

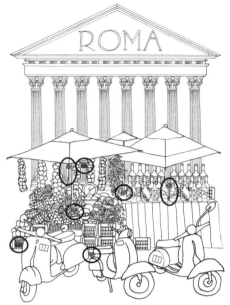

Plate 20
Butterfly (2), Crown, Heart,
Padlock, Shell, Shield

Plate 21
Crown (2), Decorative Key (2),
Heart (3)

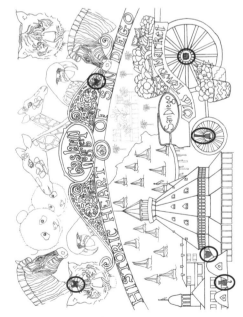

Plate 22
Bell, Butterfly (2), Cat,
Clock, Shield,

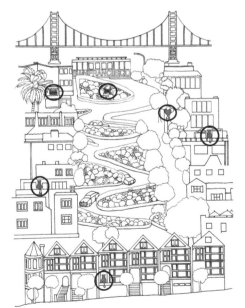

Plate 23
Butterfly, Cat (3), Crown, Heart

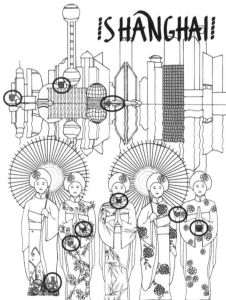

Plate 24
Butterfly (2), Cat, Clock, Heart (2),
Shell, Shield, Round Key

Plate 25
Bell, Cat, Crown, Decorative Key (2),
Russian Doll (2)

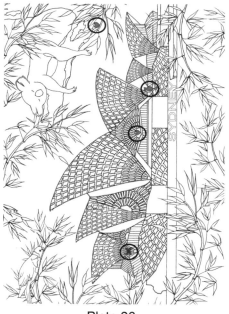

Plate 26
Butterfly, Cat, Heart (2)

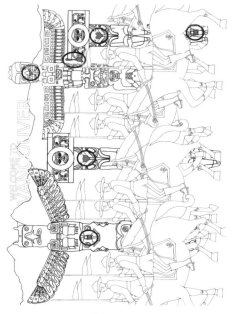

Plate 27
Bell, Heart, Padlock (2), Shield (2)

Plate 28
Decorative Key, Cat, Crown (2),
Heart, Shield,

DREAM DOODLES

Doodled within the pages of this book are:

4 Stepping Stones

4 Dragonflies

4 Snails

4 Leaves

4 Lady Bugs

6 Bees

5 Mushrooms

4 Tea Cups

4 Caterpillars

4 Lotus Flowers

10 Suns

4 Doves

4 Feathers

5 Hummingbirds

4 Butterflies

3 Frogs

48

SOLUTIONS FOR DREAM DOODLES

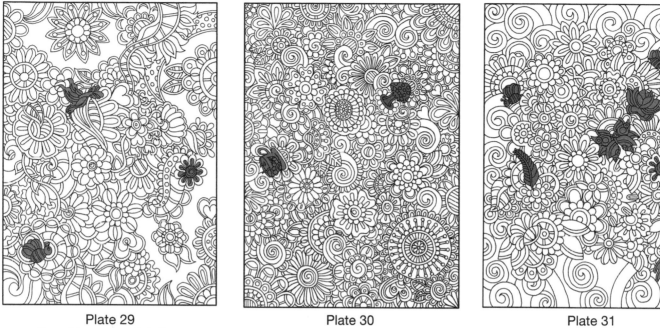

Plate 29
Bee, Hummingbird, Sun

Plate 30
Mushroom, Tea Cup

Plate 31
Bee (2), Lotus Flower, Butterfly,
Sun, Feather, Leaf

Plate 32
No Hidden Items

Plate 33
Sun, Caterpillar

Plate 34
Caterpillar, Tea Cup,
Stepping Stone, Bee

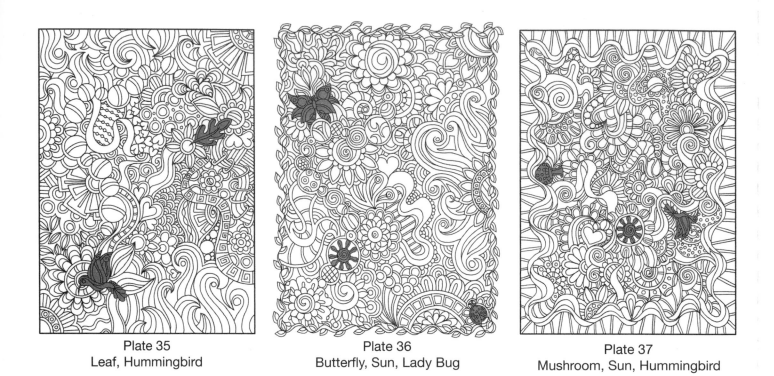

Plate 35
Leaf, Hummingbird

Plate 36
Butterfly, Sun, Lady Bug

Plate 37
Mushroom, Sun, Hummingbird

Plate 38
Mushroom, Snail

Plate 39
Dragonfly, Hummingbird

Plate 40
Leaf, Sun

DREAM DOODLES

Plate 41
No Hidden Items

Plate 42
Frog, Dragonfly

Plate 43
Hummingbird, Lotus Flower, Leaf

Plate 44
Snail, Mushroom, Frog

Plate 45
Sun, Feather, Lady Bug

Plate 46
No Hidden Items

DREAM DOODLES

61

SOLUTIONS FOR WONDROUS NATURE

Plate 57
Woodpecker feather, wasp (2), beetle (2), snail shell

Plate 58
Spider, spoon (2), bee, ant

Plate 59
Caterpillar, apple, peacock feather (2), four-leaf clover

Plate 60
Ladybug (2), key, four-leaf clover (2)

Plate 61
Mushroom (2), snail shell, teacup, (2), beetle

Plate 62
Spoon (2), key (2), snail shell, apple, acorn

Plate 63
Owl feather (2) acorn (2), ant, key

Plate 64
Woodpecker feather (2), spider, peacock feather, bee

Plate 65
Caterpillar (2), wasp, owl feather

Plate 66
Caterpillar, peacock feather (2), bee (2), acorn

Plate 67
Snail shell (2), acorn (2), spoon (2)

Plate 68
Teaspoon, teacup (2), mushroom, acorn, apple

WONDROUS NATURE

Plate 69
Woodpecker feather (2), beetle (2), owl feather, teacup

Plate 70
Mushroom, ladybug (2), spider, apple (2), acorn

Plate 71
Caterpillar, ant (2), key, mushroom (2)

Plate 72
Bee (2), owl feather, wasp, ant, spider

Plate 73
Wasp (2), four-leaf clover, ladybug (2), spider

Plate 74
Spoon (2), key (3), caterpillar (2)

WONDROUS NATURE

Plate 75
Caterpillar, apple, mushroom (2), bee

Plate 76
Bee (2), caterpillar (2), acorn

Plate 77
Caterpillar (2), spoon, ant, woodpecker feather, owl feather

Plate 78
Acorn, apple (2), spoon (3)

Plate 79
Owl feather (2), bee, snail shell (2), key.,Ladybug

Plate 80
Ladybug, peacock feather (3), beetle, ant

WONDROUS NATURE

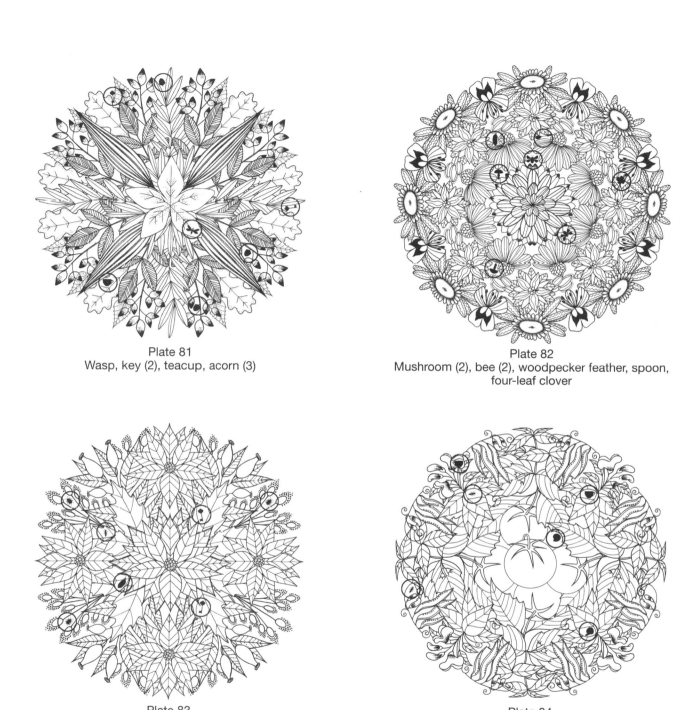

Plate 81
Wasp, key (2), teacup, acorn (3)

Plate 82
Mushroom (2), bee (2), woodpecker feather, spoon,
four-leaf clover

Plate 83
Ant, beetle (3), owl feather, key (2)

Plate 84
Apple, Snail Shell, Ant (2), Teacup (2)

WONDROUS NATURE

89

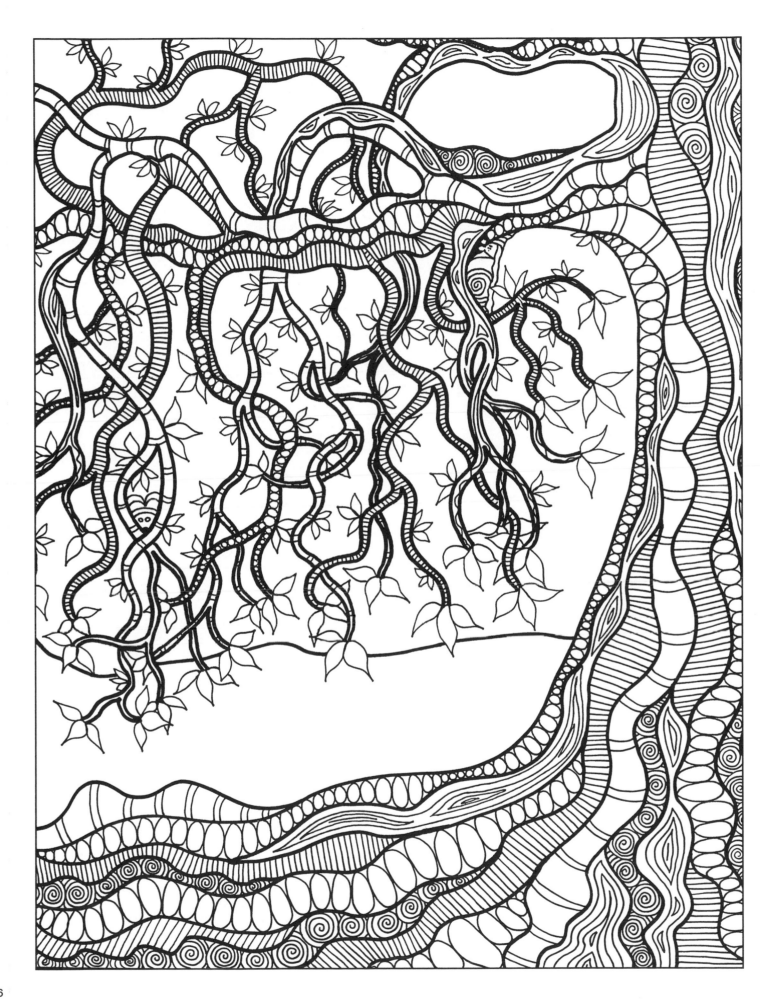

SOLUTIONS FOR INTO THE WOODS

Plate 85

Plate 87

Plate 89

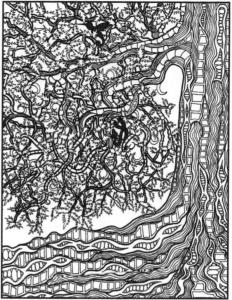

Plate 86

Plate 88

Plate 90

Plate 91

Plate 92

Plate 93

Plate 94

Plate 95

Plate 96

INTO THE WOODS